# The Heavenly Dog Father 2

## PRAYER BOOK

## LARA MAGALLON

***The Heavenly Dog Father 2***

Lara Magallon

ISBN: 978-0-578-32165-3

Copyright © 2021 All rights reserved

Published by Lara Magallon

The contents and cover of this book may not be reproduced in whole or in part in any form without the express written consent of the author.

Cover photo: Peanut, the inspiring one-eyed dog that survived a car crash. Photo by Conrad Herring

Printed in the United States of America

## I Shall Gather Up

I shall
Gather up
All the lost souls
That Wander this earth
All the ones that are alone
All the ones that are broken
All the ones that never really fitted in
I shall gather them all up
And together we shall find our home

Athey Thompson

# DEDICATION

To those special souls who have a heart that beats in the velvet folds with the rhythm of kindness and gentleness towards humanity and animals.

To those who believed in me and never once wavered.

They watched me tossed about in the storm and never doubted.

They threw me a life raft glistening with hope.

They truly knew what my heart was about.

And it was to spread love.

"Be A Rainbow In Someone's Cloud."
—Maya Angelou

# Acknowledgements

In the deepest gratitude to Paula Stein, Michele Magallon, Linda Waller, Jim Dovel, Lee Benton, Lonnie Hughes, Julie Richmond, Romano Quattropanetti, Conrad Herring, Keith Furrow, Angelo Pizelo, Steve Golden, Nancy Priestly, Matt DeMeyer, Mark Brown, Ryan and Julia Mock, Jordan and Taylor Mock, Carol Richardson, Dan and Kevin Mock, Kelly Mock, George Noujaim, John Mills, Bill Lawton, Jennifer Sohl, Tom Schenck, and my editor, Robert Goodman (Silvercat)

And a special thank you to all those contributors who scooped out their hearts and shared their dogs' prayers. You helped make *The Heavenly Dog Father 2* book what it is: an incredibly beautiful book. Thank you to all my social media friends. You have truly enriched my life and made me so much wiser. At times when I would scratch my head and wonder about my life's purpose, I would get a beautiful supportive message from someone telling me to keep going and that I was on the right path.

And many heavenly blessings to those beautiful babies who have crossed over the Rainbow Bridge: Granny, Bandit, Shadow, Nala, Jack, Raven, and many more.

In loving memory of Diane Street, Jeannette D'Arcy, Florencia Magallon, and Wayne Richardson. Each one of you lighted my way.

You made me, me.

# Little Kisses
## For: Mommy

Dear Heavenly Dog Father,

Please tell my mommy I dream of her pink kisses on my white head that Dr. Proulx the oncologist used to ask about when I visited him twice a week for my radiation. Everyone at CVS Angel Care Cancer Center said I was such a brave soul. Remember?

Every week I felt like a kindergartener heading to school meeting people who would make me get all better. But it didn't quite happen the way we intended.

Heavenly Dog Father do not forget to tell mommy that I miss her homemade carrot cake. Did you know she used to make it every year for my birthday? Carrot cake was one of the last things I ate before I left to rejoin you and play with all the dogs in heaven. I loved her homemade spaghetti too!

But most of all. I miss my mommy. Please let her know that in a warm and fuzzy dream. I am in heaven now and I am safe, strong, and healthy. I no longer have cancer. Remind mommy that she has an important job to do on earth. And that is to save dog's lives. Beware, I am watching from above to make sure she is doing it.

Love,

Granny (Boomer)

# That Miss Angel Jeannette!
### For: My Mommy

Dear Heavenly Dog Father,

Why did you trick me when you sent Miss Angel Jeannette to my mommy before I died? The day I touched nose to nose with her before I left to rejoin you in heaven, you said she was super nice! Well, she is not! In fact, she came blanketed with so many insecurities of every sort imaginable, I can't even see straight. And on top of that she is as blind as a bat, thin as a rail and as deaf as can be.

Even if I sat and counted all her ominous issues with my four paws I still could not keep up! Heavenly Dog Father is it too late to return her back to the rescue? On second thought… I bet if mommy returned her to the "rescue" little "miss smartie pants" would be caught an unending "rescue "revolving door. So, I guess we are stuck with her.

Meanwhile, Miss Angel Jeannette keeps all the dogs laughing up in heaven! Entertaining us by her nonstop barking that all the neighbors in a five-mile radius complain about.

Love,

Granny (Boomer)

# **Shadow's Prayer**
### Written with Love & Adoration by Lee Benton
### Actress/Producer/Evangelist
### Lee Benton Ministries International

Dear Heavenly Dog Father,

Isn't it funny that your name is spelled "dog" backwards? You really are the "DOG Father".

First and foremost, with all due respect, I want to lick your face and say, THANK YOU for giving me the best human Mommy and Daddy I could ever ask for. You know the first year of my life was not the easiest. Only you know how terrified and lonely I was going to the shelter not once, but TWICE before being adopted by Laura DeFalco (my Mommy's dear friend). She was super great and really nice to me, but when Mommy and Daddy watched me for two weeks while Laura was on vacation, I fell in love with them and their fur babies! I'm so glad their huskies, Starlight and Shadow, loved me and wanted me to join their family too. They asked me to be their brother! Only you, Dog Father, could have made that possible. We had so much fun playing together, and it was really kind of Laura to let my Mommy and Daddy adopt me, so we could stay together. Thank you!

I also want to thank you for helping my parents to get me approved to be a SERVICE DOG! Because of that, I get to dress up and be of service to the sweetest people at the Senior Living Homes and the cutest kids at the Children's Quadriplegic Hospital. They love to hold and pet me with the biggest smiles on their faces. I hope they know that

they put the biggest smile on MY face! I pray that you give the elderly peace every day and comfort knowing that you are with them. I pray that the children get to move as you intended their bodies to move. I believe in miracles. I pray that you heal them and give them so many more smiles. I hope to make them smile again when I get a chance to visit. I love them so much, and I hope they know how much YOU love them EVEN MORE!

Dog Father, if I can pray now for myself, please heal my kidneys. I was diagnosed with kidney disease. As you know, I may be small, but I am a mighty, fearless, 12-lb. Papillon Mix at the ripe age of 14. I am doing my best to be brave and courageous during this time. I pray that you make my nauseous tummy go away, so I can enjoy my food again. I know the fluid IV's are good for me, but I don't like the needles. I want to be healthy, and I want Mommy and Daddy to not look so sad around me especially when we see the doctor. I miss having the energy that I used to have, which always made Mommy and Daddy smile. I love how they giggle when I perk up and play with my fur brother and sister, Spirit and Starlight, and enjoy our hikes together. Thank you for Starlight and Spirit. Thank you that they're the best fur sister and brother I could ever wish for! Starlight tries to watch over me like a momma even though I'm older than her, and Spirit is exactly like his name - full of SPIRIT! I know you love them so much like I do! Thank you that they keep me on my toes and have so much fun with me! I love them so, so much. My holistic/GP Doctor, David Gordon, at Arch Beach Veterinarian Clinic in Laguna Beach, CA, is the best, and I'm so grateful for him and his staff who all love and care for me and my siblings. But, Dog Father, can you please make me healthier? I

will never give up, and I will fight every day to be with Mommy, Daddy, Starlight, and Spirit as long as I can. If you can help me win this fight sooner, I'd appreciate it.

When it's my time, and I trust that you know exactly when that is, I pray that it'll be a nice homecoming on the other side of the Rainbow Bridge. Waiting for me, will be my other husky brothers and sister, Kuma, Paris, and Blue, including little Pooh Bear, the cutest teddy bear chow-chow. Mommy talks about them all the time, and I imagine they are SO MUCH FUN to play with just like Starlight and Spirit! Mommy talks about her and Daddy's mansion in Heaven, and I know my fur siblings will take me there, so we can play and wait together until the whole family is reunited again, someday.

Until then, Dog Father, please give me energy to win this fight every day and give all my family perfect health, so we can spend more days playing and smiling on earth until I earn my wings.

 Amen with kisses on your face, Dog Father! I love you!

SHADOW

The Dog Who Never Gave Up

Shadow is so loved by his Mommy & Daddy - Lee Benton & David Hrisca

# To My Mom

**For: Julie Richmond**
**Staff Writer At House of Destiny Music**

Dear Heavenly Dog Father,

Momma, I just want to thank you for giving me a home.

A little five-pound poodle scared and all alone.

I was already ten when you took me in.

Wow, we had some happy times then,

Dad, gram, and my little sister you called friend.

I know now that you cry a lot for all that you have lost.

If you only knew how sad that makes me because I want you to laugh & smile.

You have your dogs that love you like I; they need you now.

Oh, and just one more thing I need to say that my Aunt Tonya needs to know.

Just today I saw Sarge, Shadow and Princess but Princess misses her sister Snow.

I told her someday she will join us, we'll all run and have so much fun.

In the meantime, always remember, you will always be my mom.

Love Fur-ever,

Your Junior Dog

# My Simple Prayers

### For: Chuck Von Yamashita

Dear Heavenly Dog Father.

 I am so grateful that dad keeps healthy so we can continue having adventures creating beautiful memories that we share. Thank you for placing me in such a wonderful adventurous home!


Love,

Paris

# Party Poodle
## For: Tom Schenck

Dear Heavenly Dog Father,

My name is Boyd Bearington III, I am a miniature poodle. As a little newborn I was hungry all the time and had to fight through my brothers and sisters to get to my mother.

With your help Heavenly Dog Father, we all started to play. My grandparents were a nice Amish Couple who seemed to be the ones feeding my mother and father, since they did not nurse anymore. One day, a genuinely nice couple came to visit me and my family. They, like others held us and kissed us, but there was something about them that seemed extra loving...and they seemed to pay more attention to me.

Heavenly Dog Father, I bet you had something to do with that! They liked the fact that I had three different colors of fur and was, therefore, a "Party Poodle "because I was unique...I found out later that they too were rather unique.

Heavenly Dog Father its now ten years since they adopted me and have filled me with love ever since. I sleep with them in their big bed. I am always closer to Nancy, wherever she goes because I sense that she needs my extra support because she is handicapped. Even when Nancy is downstairs in her wheelchair, I always sit on her lap. I guard over her just like what I know you would want me to do.

They are such a loving family with two special sons who like to pet me too. I am one of the lucky animals who found a great home and I guess they are lucky too to get a "Party Poodle" like me.  Thank you once again Heavenly Dog Father for my wonderful life with Tom, Nancy, Gable and Hagan. Maybe one day I can help you train the dogs up in Heaven. What do you think?

Love,

Boyd

# Babe Is Here!
## For: Jim Dovel

Dear Heavenly Dog Father!

Your little girl Babe here, although my Dad called me baby! I sure want to Thank You for finding a loving Mom and Dad for me! That fire was really scary, and my old owners only barely left the door open so I could escape! I ran and ran until I found myself in a neighborhood with houses but no people! Finally, a white truck picked me up and took me to a place with lots of other dogs. They all told me how scary the fire was. My new Mom and Dad came one day, and I barked and barked to get their attention, I didn't know they didn't like too much barking, but they picked me anyhow! Lucky for me they took me home to their house and I got lots of food and treats because they said I was sooooo small. My Dad even let me go to Aunt Donnas for Thanksgiving and I got turkey and everything! I know my Dad was really upset when you brought me back to be with you. We only got six years together, but they were the best years a little girl could ever want. Heavenly Dog Father, please protect my Dad, during his surgery I did my best to help, but the war was coming back to hurt him again!

Make this the last surgery please!

Your little girl Babe!

# Have Faith
### For: Steve Golden

Dear Heavenly Dog Father,

Please let my owner Steve know that I am with him always! His love for me is and will be forever a part of my spiritual energy. I run next to him and walk by his side always.

When I was on the earthly plain, I was blessed to be his dog. As you witnessed Heavenly Dog Father, we spent all our time together. I Love You.

Thank you,

Rozzi

# I Adore You
## For: Nancy

Dear Heavenly Dog Father,

My name is Merlin,

I am a Brown and White Chihuahua Doggie Love. Even though I am small, I have an excessively big heart! I am very blessed with a good life and a family that loves and adores me. I am so grateful for their kindness.

I love to turn upside down and have my tummy rubbed and my heart kissed.

Heavenly Dog Father, you were so wise when you brought me back on earth. My family loves it when I roll over and lay upside down with my feet in the air. Either Nancy or her son Tom will come over and laugh and play with me while kissing my heart and rubbing my tummy. Can you tell I love it by the fierce wagging of my tail?

I am grateful that they give me fresh meat and good food and clean water. Heavenly Dog Father, if it super delicious I share it with you too.

You can see I get so sad when everyone goes out and I am home alone. I sit on the arm of the sofa and look out the window and try to be patient to await their return. Sometimes I feel they are gone from me for too long.

Heavenly Dog Father, when they return, they can see how happy I am to see them, and I forget all my sadness. I run to the door and bark with excitement and wait for them to pick me up and love me up.

Thank You so much dear Heavenly Dog Father for such a wonderful family. I am so grateful!

Love,

Merlin

# **Stella's Thoughts**
### For: Steve Ronce

Oh! Heavenly Dog Father,

Thank you for giving me a loving home. I know there are many dogs going homeless and killed for no other reason but stupidity! My name is Stella. I am a nine-year-old Great Dane Oh! Heavenly Dog Father. I have plenty of food in my loving home and everything I could possibly want!

I praise you Oh Heavenly Dog Father! May other dogs find and have the same as I do! That is my prayer to you Oh Heavenly Dog Father! Please make it happen soon! Amen

Love,

Stella

# KISSES FROM SMOKEY
### For: Kathleen McKee

DEAR MOM,

DEAR HEAVENLY DOG FATHER,

I'LL NEVER FORGET OUR BEGINNING AND MY LIFE WITH MY NEW MOM.

MY OTHER MOM PUT ME ON A WILD DOG RANCH AND WHEN THAT DIDN'T WORK OUT YOU CAME AND GOT ME. I WENT FROM MY OLD MOM'S ARMS INTO YOURS. IT WAS THE BEST HUG AND THE SAFEST PLACE I'D EVER BEEN. DO YOU REMEMBER SEEING THAT HEAVENLY DOG FATHER? I THOUGHT I SAW YOU SHEDDING A TEAR.

FINALLY, I KNEW I WAS HOME. I GOT THE BEST FOOD AND CARE FOR SO MANY YEARS AND I REMEMBER YOU BRUSHING MY LONG FUR AND CLEANING MY EARS AND ALWAYS FILLING MY DISH WITH GOOD YUMMY FOOD. WHEN I GOT SICK YOU LEARNED HOW TO GIVE ME SHOTS AND FOR YEARS, I LIVED A LONG AND HAPPY LIFE.

I WOULD SIT RIGHT CLOSE TO MY MOM ON THE COUCH WITH A WARM FIRE. I KNEW THAT WHEN I WAS SO CLOSE, I'D ALWAYS BE SAFE-- AND I WAS.

HEAVENLY DOG FATHER WHEN YOU LET MOM KNOW MY LAST DAYS WERE COMING, WE WOULD

STROLL THROUGH OUR TROPICAL GARDENS AND ENJOY THE SWEET SAFE OCEAN AIR THEN RETURN HOME.

EVEN AFTER I WENT TO JOIN YOU, HEAVENLY DOG FATHER, SHE CONTINUED TO FILL MY DISH. BECAUSE OF HER LOVING SPIRIT, MY SPIRIT LIVED IN MY EARTH BODY FOR A VERY LONG TIME.

HEAVENLY DOG FATHER PLEASE LET HER KNOW THAT I AM ALWAYS WITH HER. I NOW WATCH OVER HER AS SHE DID ME. MY BIG GREEN EYES NEVER LOST SIGHT OF HER ON EARTH AND NEVER DO HERE IN HEAVEN.

ONE DAY MOM WE WILL BE TOGETHER AGAIN AND OUR SPIRITS WILL NOT BE SEPARATE. HEAVENLY DOG FATHER WHEN MOM HEARS MY BARK, PLEASE LET HER KNOW THAT IT'S ME "SMOKEY" WHO LIVES ETERNALLY AND WAITS FOR HER RETURN.

LOVE,

SMOKEY

# Life Is Not The Same Without You.
### Fr: Linda Waller

Dear Heavenly Dog Father,

Tell my mom Linda,

Don't cry for me for I am still here.

Inside your heart where you hold me dear.

Thank you for the lovely life we had

I wish it had been longer, but I am still glad.

Remember the good times mummy full of love,

And know I'm still here just a little way above. Love you mummy and I know you love me.

Love,

Your Boy Jack

# My Family
### For: Maria Sinclair

Dear Heavenly Dog Father,

My name is Ozzy I'm a jack cross mix and my human Maria always said my cute face was all Jack Russell and the rest of me was more like a beagle. She's always told me I'm a gorgeous unique boy. I've had a long and amazing life. My mummy Bonnie only had 2 pups that was me and my brother Joesph. We had an auntie called Honey too. Our human Maria promised us we would be all kept together as a family. I loved my family we had fun playing and chasing each other. As us puppies grew up Maria took us all together runs through woods and beaches. We would swim in lakes and the sea. Even you Heavenly Dog Father jumped into swim!

We all liked to be kept busy or we would be bored and chew up our humans' shoes and even the door once. We were always forgiven as our human Maria loved us and called us her best friends. I loved to cuddle up with Maria most of all I liked to be by her side always and not let her out of my sight or I would be so destressed. I would cry and bark until we were all together again.

 As you already know Heavenly Dog Father, the years went by and the first to go to heaven was my auntie Honey. I was so incredibly sad and cuddled into my human even closer. Honey was such a fantastic auntie to me, and I missed her. It was my mummy, brother and I left to get on with life. We never forgot honey though she was a special little lady. Maria started her own family after a few years. The little humans were fun and loved us too. The house became noisier, but the tiny humans were always great for sneaking extra snacks and cuddles. Life was perfect and then one awful night my mummy Bonnie went to heaven she was old but us 2 boys felt so lost and confused. Maria said she was now our mom and promised our mummy Bonnie this as she passed away peacefully in her arms. Us boys were 14 at this point so not so young now neither I could see the worry in mom's eyes about this.

Last year my brother and best friend Joesph suddenly got sick. Mom had to take him to the vet, but mom came home alone. She lifted me up with tears in her eyes explaining Joesph was now with my mummy Bonnie and auntie Honey rejoining you Heavenly Dog Father. I had my human mom and the tiny humans, but I felt so sad I was the only one left in my dog family.

I overheard mom quietly telling you Heavenly Dog Father that she could see my own health leaving me from the day my brother joined the others in heaven. My legs no longer worked the same and I felt so tired and sore. Mom knew I was getting sick and when we went to the vet, I was so scared. Mom wasn't allowed to stay as there was something called Coronavirus. The vet ran different tests and exams. I cried and peed on myself in fear. I didn't want to go to heaven, yet I loved my human family and wanted to go home. However, Heavenly Dog Father when I saw you watching over me that gave me great peace.

I was so happy when mom came back for me and bolted to our car as fast as my old legs could go. Mom has told me I'm on borrowed time I have cancer and I see her sneaking medications into my food. I take it because I want to live a little yet. I know Heavenly Dog Father you get such a kick out of watching the tiny humans push me about on my pushchair now. We go to all the woods, forests, and parks I use to run through with my dog family. Everyone hugs me lots and spoils me with food.

Dear Heavenly Dog Father, when mom and I are alone she cries a lot, her tears roll down my fur. I try to lick as many tears away as I can. I wish I could speak if only a few words... can you possibly comfort her? I would tell my mom not to be sad and as much as I will miss my human family, I will be with my mummy Bonnie, you, auntie honey and brother Joesph again. Please let her know that.

Soon I will be pain free and young again rejoining you dear Heavenly Dog father and we will chase each other through woods and swim in beautiful lakes. I would tell her thank you and I will always love you.

Love, Ozzy

# **Thankfulness**
## For: David Irvin

Dear Heavenly Dog Father-- hi!

This is jasmine. I'm kinda tired right now. Me and daddy and you have been playing throw and fetch. So, while I rest, I wanted to say hello and to thank you. Daddy says we should always be thankful for all you do for us. But he seems worried about a lot of crazy stuff going on this year. That is what he calls it. Crazy stuff. I am not for sure what he means, except that one month when my sisters Tessa and Mollie left us to be with you at that "rainbow bridge" thing daddy talks about. We were extra sad then. But daddy says it is better to be with the Heavenly Dog Father than to stay here! Wow!! I can't wait to go visit you! Thanks for loving doggies so much!

Daddy always gives thanks to you Heavenly Dog Father for things when he prays. And he asks you watch over me and him and mommy. I guess he means you watch us when we play together or go for rides in mommy's van. That's pretty neat! So, I thank you for my toys and snackies--specially the snackies, hahaha! And thanks for mommy and daddy, and my bestest cousin Patches! We look the same, except he is black and white. Daddy calls him skunk boy! That's funny, huh?

Thank you thank you thank you Heavenly Dog Father! That's in case I forgotten anything. We sure love you. Say hi to Tessa and Mollie-oh, and missy too. She came to see you last year. Well...love and slurpy kisses! Amen.


Love and kisses,

Jasmine

# My Angel
### For: Pam Butman

Dear Heavenly Dog Father,

Thank you for bringing angel into my life.

When we very first got our little angel, we had brought her to our friend's house and after a little while - she had become frightened about something -she came to me, looking up at me with those eyes needing my protection. Now I have never been a mom so didn't know what that was like, to protect something so priceless. I put her in my arms and kissed her. My heart grew to an immeasurable size that moment. And it's grown bigger every moment since that day...

Thank you,

Pamela Butman and my Angel

Ps. Angel told me that she talks to you every day Heavenly Dog Father and you give her great practical advice on how to be a good little doggie.

# My Heart In Form Of A Dog

**For: June Richards**

Dear Heavenly Dog Father,

I'm praying for my mommy's healing. See mommy has a bad Knee and Hip. Her hip is gone. Mommy is going to try shots and Physical therapy for a while but if that doesn't work, she will have to have surgery. Which mommy doesn't want!

So Heavenly Dog Father, I am asking you to touch my Mommy And heal her with shots and therapy work. Also, Heavenly Dog Father they told Mommy we needed to move into an apartment for Disabled and Handicapped people to be on the ground floor with no steps.

So, I'm asking you to please let something come soon. See mommy can hardly get up steps or step in the tub take a shower. We really need this! Drs are working on it right now and mommy just got a letter from the Dr.

So please answer my prayer. Heavenly Dog Father. In your name Amen.

Love,

Miss Dakota

# My Loving Fur Babies
### For: Tammy King

Dear Heavenly Dog Father,

My mama Tammy is so funny! She makes me happy! She plays with me and my toys and hugs me all the time which I love! Mommy slept with me one time on the floor when I was sick, and it was hard for me to get off the bed. She wanted to make sure I was ok.

Most of the time we ride in a taxi to the vet to take care of me whenever I am sick or need a checkup. I sure love my mama and my grandma and aunt Tina. When I sleep with momma it makes me so happy and I love the treats. Heavenly Dog Father you can see that I am very spoiled.

Love,

Kojack

# My Love For Mom
### For: Sharon Pallister

Dear Heavenly Dog Father,

When mum and dad rescued my fur sister Betty, I was a bit unsure but soon realized they had enough love for both of us. Our first outing as a family was to one of my favourite places the river with the waterfalls. I knew where to go and led Betty to the bestest fun places. We explored the riverbank together and enjoyed the mud, I like mud, but Betty was a lady and didn't want to get her paws dirty. We trotted in the shallow water, again Betty wasn't keen, I could see she was safe with mum, so I dragged dad into the river for a good splodge oh I love a good old soaking. When I got out, I had a good old shake, well I wanted to share the water with everyone. By the time we got back to the car I was covered in mud just how I like it. Betty was nice and clean and only needed her paws wiping whereas me, as usual, looked like a little urchin lol but I like being rubbed down with a towel. Mum wrapped us both up in blankets and my new fur sister cuddled up to me in the car and went to sleep. As a new big brother, I thought let her sleep this is my job to make her feel safe, mum was in tears but happy tears like the ones on the day she became my mummy, because we had bonded quickly, and we looked so cute. Happy days. Thank you so much Heavenly Dog Father!

Faithfully,

Koda

# I Am Always There With You
### For: Docteures Giselle

(Dear Heavenly Dog Father Help The Mommy To Know)

Since the beginning of our journey together

I knew you were my "Special Mother."

When they told you I was sickly and to take me back

You looked at the Boy and kept me as a part of your Family Pack.

You nursed me back to health and I felt so good

As you'd rub my hips, I'd stand still because I understood

I was a German Shepherd Puppy born to run so fast.

You made sure that I was well taken care of and LOVED, what a blast!

Our Family trips together were both short and long.

You made me learn that I'd have to get along

With the Boys Cats, his Lizards and never give in

To that great urge I'd have to make them run and hide again and again.

We shopped together for my favorite toys.

I'd get treats, the largest bone, toys that squeaked of the joys

They brought me, both inside and out.

Our Family was FUN without a doubt.

Know that I am there with you when you drive at night.

I was by your side when you were battling to stay alive with all your might.

I stay with you to help guide you throughout the day.

I am with you knowing you hear and feel me in a way

That is hard to describe…yet you know it's true.

I AM ALWAYS there with you.

"Shane Doggy"

# I Love My Mom

### For: Lynda Weelans
### (In loving memory of Lynda)

Dear Heavenly Dog Father,

Let me introduce myself, I am Bella. I am a 4.5-year-old English Bulldog. I live in Colorado, originally from Wyoming. I have many fun and blessed memories. I love being with my Mum. I faithfully follow her everywhere and if she must go somewhere without me, I sit at the door and whine until she returns. Heavenly Dog Father do you remember that day when I was a puppy a big dog came running across a courtyard at me and Mum while we were out walking?

 My Mum grabbed me up quickly and faced a brick wall to protect me. She kept me safe as the dog nipped at her back until finally leaving. At that point in time, I knew how loved I was and that my Mum would keep me safe at any cost. We have had many fun adventures driving in the car and visiting family and friends. My Mum takes me and my older fur sister, Minnie everywhere she can and know that she loves me as much as I love her. I hope all my fur friends are as blessed as I am. Thank you dear Heavenly Dog Father for placing me in such a loving home.

Love,

Bella

# Ravens Prayer
### For: Jim Dovel

Dear Heavenly Dog Father

Well today was a tough day for my Dad! You wanted me in heaven, but I did not know how to tell my Dad! He saw my face and I gave him that look that you taught me! He took a few hours to understand but I could tell by the handkerchief that it was hard for him to call the Vet. I have been sick for a long time, but the Vet did not catch it until late last year. The good news is that I get to see my brother Buddy, he sure was fun to play with!

Also, I was really looking forward to our trip to Florida and all the parks Mom and Dad and I were going to see!

Your girl,

Raven

# Magics Heavenly Prayer
### For: Scott Marple

LORD I KNOW I MAY NOT BE HERE MUCH LONGER AND I KNOW WHEN I GO MY DADDY WILL FALL APART IN HEARTACHE. PLEASE LOOK OVER HIM LIKE HIS LOVING HEART LOOKED OVER ME ALL THOSE YEARS KEEPING ME HAPPY AND SOOO LOVED GOING FOR RIDES TAKING ME SWIMMING, ALWAYS GIVING ME TREATS. I PRAY LORD THAT MY DADDY AND I ARE RE-UNITED ON THE OTHER SIDE OF THAT RAINBOW BRIDGE I KNOW THAT'S WHAT HE DESIRES AND MY SPIRIT WILL ALWAYS BE WITH HIM, I PRAY THAT HE FINDS THAT MATE THAT WILL LOVE HIM LIKE I DID, I WATCHED HIM GET HURT A LOT AND HE ALMOST DIED IN 2007 UNFORTUNATELY I WON'T BE THERE FOR HIM TO LICK HIS TEARS AWAY AND COMFORT HIM. PLEASE LORD LOOK OVER HIM AND MAKE HIS LIFE A HAPPY ONE,

IN YOUR NAME I PRAY AMEN

LOVE,

MAGIC.

# The Biller Six Pack!
## For: Coral Biller

Dear Heavenly Dog Father,

We are The Biller 6 Pack and we would like to Thank You for our wonderful family. Our Daddy Jason Biller & Mommy Coral Biller spend their life trying to make us so happy. We have gone through some very happy and sad times together, and not one day goes by that the 6 of us do not feel all the love from our Daddy and Mommy, they make sure of it! Thank You so much God for your plan, it is your plan and your will that put us with such a wonderful family. We have our own bedroom fully furnished including a king size bed and every toy we could possibly want, but most importantly we are SO RICH WITH LOVE!!

We Thank You and Praise You Lord every single day for the blessing of our FAMILY!

In Your Precious Name We Pray Lord

Amen.

Love Always, The Biller 6 Pack

Daddy Atari, Mama Lyli, Rayne, Dodge, Twizle and Gizzy

# Our Beautiful Mommy

### For: Andrea Bunny Corleto

Dear Heavenly Dog Father,

Mum we love you so much. We follow you everywhere and can't help it. Snuggling on the couch or at bedtime with you is great! You take such good care of us. We get to run and play in the big yard. In the summer we jump in the pools you put out for us.

Toys and bones are some of our very favorite things. We often ask the Heavenly Dog Father what would we do without you? When you come home, we look out the door for you.... Sometimes we have to run out, down the steps and whimper and wag tails.

We just started a new daily chorus time. All 4 of us sing, howl happily together... Heavenly Dog Father can you and the dogs hear us in heaven?

We Love everyone in our family but you especially Mum Andrea. Always with you in our hearts forever.

Thank you, dear Heavenly Dog Father, for being so clever and placing us in such a loving home.

From the loves of your life.

Baby, Elsa, Babydoll & that Duck (Lobo)

These dogs are the only loves of my life. I care more about them than myself.

# JIS Master

**For: Raman, Raman's Ark**

DEAR HEAVENLY DOG FATHER,

A LITTLE DOGGIE PRAYER FOR HIS MASTER.

A MASTER WHO IS FIRM AND KIND AND UNDERSTANDS A DOGGIE'S MIND, A WALKIE AND A MEAL EACH DAY THATS ALL I ASK FOR WHEN I PRAY.

LOVE,

MAGGIE, MILLIE, MIA AND MISTY

# Precious It's Hard To Kiss Goodbye And It's Ok To Cry

**For: Keith Furrow**

Dear Mother Father God,

Thank you for this Precious puppy. She has been a great companion and my best friend for many many years. I ask in the name of Jesus for you to send your angels to surround and lift up our family in this sacred and challenging time. I pray that this Precious girl has the happiest and longest life possible. That she feels peace as her Spirit makes its transition to heaven. I surrender her to you Holy Spirit. I ask you in Jesus' name, that when she experiences her last breath; that you send your angels to surround her and comfort. Godspeed on her journey to glory. I know I will see her again and will look for her, at the foot of that glorious rainbow bridge.

Amen and so it.

Love, Keith

# I Am Nemo
### For: Rainer Kilian

Dear Heavenly Dog Father,

I am Nemo, the Dragon Dog, the Poet and Philosopher dog

I am up here, I crossed the rainbow bridge

I don't know a GOD, up here is no GOD up here are just all the souls, that left earth

I do not even know if here is up or where we are the souls here are all happy, they all LOVE each other there is no hate, no greed, no hunger, no pain all is joyful, free, all play and it is full of LOVE but where is GOD, that old man with the long beard? No one here has a body as they used to have on earth there is no age, just pure LOVE and light but the light isn't too bright, that it hurts it is bright and smooth the same time it is embracing and even though it is bright it is very warm, making you feel like in your mother's womb and this feeling that is all over the place this feeling, making you feel good and soothing even you look at someone that did hurt you on earth Forgiveness, LOVE, Calmness, I think that is GOD.

GOD, he or she or whatever, is in us, we feel it, if not on earth, we feel it up here doesn't matter if you believe in a religious version of GOD or if you just believe in LOVE itself because it is equal LOVE is GOD, if you find the

LOVE in yourself, you find GOD believe in whatever you believe about GOD or even many GODs is you will see it once we meet again

So my prayer as the Dragon Dog for my humans, no, for all humans is as follows...

Find the LOVE inside yourself so you find your own inner self GOD

Love And Kisses,

Nemo

# My Beloved Bandit Donald & Susan Turner

### Donald Susan

Dear Heavenly Dog Father,

 This is just a little reminder to my mom and daddy on earth I feel your presence and see you every day from across the rainbow bridge even though I miss y'all so much especially my little sister Zoe, but now I'm cancer free and I am not in pain anymore, I will always be your little angel no matter what. You gave me the best 17 years on earth that a fur baby could have ever ask for I remember when y'all came to get me in Tennessee left me in car alone with Anthony's Mexican food and I see a good bite for me and it made me so sick peppers and onions lol. Anthony never let me live that one down I always loved traveling.  I will never forget about daddy sneaking me in a hotel in a suitcase that zipped from top and mommy said leave it open so I can breathe till you get to room and I popped my little head out no one seen me with y'all to Branson Missouri to get Andy's custard pup cones my favorite place. Mom you always made my birthday parties special with a big party cupcakes even my aunt Rhonda came to photography it I felt so special.  Mom you know how storms always scared me well we don't have storms here I'm thankful GOD put Ricardo in our lives, I was a bit jealous to start off but GOD sent him for Zoe so she would not be left alone. Love y'all see you soon one day I'm waiting on y'all.

Love,

Bandit Turner

# To My Mom,
## By Darci to her Mom Jill

Dear Heavenly Dog Father,

The things I want to tell you while there is still time

I love the way you call me "sweet pea" even at 3:00 am when it is still snowing in May

I love you for my Winnie ducks, they are my comfort animals

I love you for sharing your breakfast with me every morning even when you are on a diet and have little to eat

I love you best of all for being my Mom and my best friend.

I love my Dad for protecting me from all the critters in the backyard, the phone noises, and taking me to see the turtles.

I am a very, very lucky little girl.

Love,

Darci

xxxooooooxxx

# **Thanks Mom**
### For: Lynn Bonham

My name is Lulu. I am 20 years old. I want to say I love you mom for giving me the best life.

Dear Heavenly Dog Father, Here's my story...

I was living on the streets in Porterville. Just a throw away dog. I was eating out of trash cans. The neighbors were tired of me making a mess. I was 9 months old. This was 2002.

I was picked up by animal control and my time at the shelter was up. My kennel card was folded for the team to dispatch me. A rescue lady named Lori saw this an pulled me into her rescue. I'm safe...I went to the vet to get spayed and all of my shots to be adopted...

I was semi feral and escaped my crate on the floor. I had popped everywhere and ran straight into a lap that looked safe. She let me up poop and all!! I was shaking and so scared and that lady is my mom, Lynn. She was taking my soon to be new sister for her rabies shot at the vet. Somehow, we touched each other's soul that day. She went home and told my new dad about me.

Valentine's day 2002 they officially adopted me!

I have never been a bad girl. Always show my gratitude, they never had to potty train me. I never hurt the cats, I never ran away or fought with any of my siblings or the 100's of fosters dogs my mom has brought home.

I taught her what a rescue is. Now she is the founding member of Russell Rescue CA.

Love you mom,

Lulu

# Love From A Paw...

**For: Lonnie Hughes, Producer of Award Allen & Gray Musical Festival**

Dear Heavenly Dog Father,

I swear "he"-my owner wants Love as much as he misses playing with me. I remember him cuddling with me when he was nine years old. He would play with my Floppy ears, and he would whisper in them "Can you hear me, cause I love you, even more than mom and dad loves me"...And I swear he did. Whatever he ate, I ate. He called me his very special "Pal". He would always tell me not to play in the street but one early morning I was running to catch a mongoose and I wasn't paying attention and my lights went out. I didn't know what happened until I was going up to meet "Heavenly Dog Father" he pointed to my ten-year-old "Owner" crying his eyes out looking over my body. To make matter's worst it was his tenth birthday. From that moment on, he closed off his human heart to love. I know he likes cooking for other humans, but I think he misses cuddling with me. So, Heavenly Dog Father could you send him a surprise little dog (a puppy) that could open his heart to love again. And maybe, this might also encourage him that it's time to find his Forever Human, perfectly designed just for him. Thank you so much for loving him and keeping him safe, all his life.

Sincerely,

A Black Chow, "Blacky"

# Thank You For Our Mommy
### From: Kym Reed Custer

Dear Heavenly Dog Father,

Thank you for bringing our mommy to us!

We do not know how she was able to do anything before you brought her into our lives.

She would let people walk their dogs by our house without saying a word. She would let the chipmunks and squirrels run amok and never chase them.

Thank you, Heavenly Dog Father, for giving mommy someone to go into the bathroom with. How could she ever have that alone time without four eyes and eight paws right there in front of her?

Mommy and Daddy thought that we should sleep in a crate but you in your infinite wisdom knew that we must be on the bed taking up all the extra space (and covers).

We can't imagine how they could sleep without us digging, snoring, and stretching our legs as far and hard as we can pushing them to the edge of the bed.

Yes, Heavenly Dog Father you have answered all of mommies' prayers and we are so grateful to you that you brought mommy to our house.

Love,

Bella and Trumpy

# Nala My Love You Has To Go Right?
## For: Romano Quattropanetti

Dear Heavenly Dog Father,

I was looking at the sea on a cold winter day sitting on a white log consumed by the water and salt when I turned my gaze on the beach. There was no trace of humans, the only sound was that of the waves breaking on the shore. An indistinct shape in the distance approached. I stared at her and when it became clear to me that it was a Beagle, I saw her trotting purposefully towards me. My heart started beating fast, but I didn't understand why. She was close to me I was struck by amazement. I recognized those eyes, that unique way of looking at me. My breath became short because I thought it couldn't be true. A moment later she was next to me and sat down with her little head on my leg. A tear dropped suddenly and fell on her. Her perfume shook me, and I gently began to caress her. Soft and warm, I had Nala with me once again.

I talked to her as I had done so many times as if that cursed December 13, 2019, had never happened. She listened to me moving his eyes to tell me I understand what you are saying as the sun began to dip into the sea. There was peace around me, there was love and joy. The time of a sunset, she licked my hand and got up, looked at the sea and I understood, I kissed her for a long time hugging her tightly and whispered, "Nala my love you have to go right?"

She stopped licking me, looked at me softly, got up and pointed towards the sea, sniffing the sand. It disappeared as it had appeared, but I saw it in the bright red horizon. I got up with my back to the sea and walked away smiling without looking back, aware that Nala is part of my essence of life.

Love,

Romano for Nala

# Nala Amore Mio Devi Andare Bene?
## Per: Romano Quattropanetti

Caro Padre Cane Celeste,

Guardavo il mare in una giornata fredda d'inverno seduto su un tronco bianco consumato dall'acqua e dalla salsedine quando volsi il mio sguardo sulla spiaggia. Non c'era traccia di umani, il solo rumore era quello delle onde che si infrangevano sul bagnasciuga. Una forma indistinta in lontananza si avvicinava. La fissai e quando mi fu chiaro che era un Beagle vidi che trotterellava decisa verso di me. Il cuore prese a battere velocemente ma non capivo il perché. Fu vicino a me fui colto dallo stupore. Riconobbi quegli occhi, quel suo modo unico di guardarmi. Il respiro si fece corto perché pensai che non poteva essere vero. Un attimo dopo era vicina a me si sedette appoggiando la sua testolina sulla mia gamba. Una lacrima mi scese improvvisa e cadde su di lei. Il suo profumo mi scosse e con delicatezza presi ad accarezzarla. Morbida e calda avevo ancora una volta Nala con me. Le parlai come avevo fatto tante volte come se quel maledetto 13 dicembre 2019 non ci fosse mai stato. Mi ascoltava muovendo i suoi occhi per dirmi capisco quello che mi dici mentre il sole iniziava ad immergersi nel mare. C'era pace intorno a me, c'era amore e gioia. Il tempo di un tramonto, mi leccò una mano e si alzò, guardò il mare ed io capii, la baciai a lungo abbracciandola forte e le sussurrai "Nala amore mio devi andare vero?" Smise di leccarmi, mi guardò dolcemente si alzò e puntò decisa il mare annusando la sabbia. Scomparve così come era apparsa ma io la vidi nell'orizzonte di un rosso acceso. Mi alzai voltando le spalle al mare e mi incamminai sorridendo senza voltarmi, consapevole che Nala fa parte della mia essenza di vita.

Amore,

Romano e Nala

# Miss Charlotte's Heart
## For: Teresa Silva, Rescuer

Dear Heavenly Dog Father,

My name is Charlotte I am 8 years old; I think I had a rough start in life, I was in a shelter, and I was out of time. My days were numbered that's when I met my hero Lynn Bonham, she saved my life! On Super Bowl Sunday 2019, Lynn took me to meet granny. I didn't like to be touched or picked up, I also despised dogs, I was very aggressive towards them. I was nervous at first, but it didn't last long.

Granny had food and water dishes, just for me. warms blanket and treats with granny telling me stories about all the adventures we would go on. One night I snuck into granny's bed... Slept all night. Now I sleep with granny every night. Granny gave me massages; it changed my life! Now I love to be touched I am almost too affectionate. I learned that love feels good! I am a very happy girl! I became more trusting over "time." I 've been on so many adventures to parks, missions, beaches, car rides meeting new friends. I got lots of treats because "I am a good girl" and granny "is so proud!" My Paw Paw loves me too. He lets me supervise whenever he works on a project. He tells me I'm "such a sweet girl" "Paw Paw's girl." He gives me treats every day! I love my Paw Paw! I am adopted now! Granny fostered a few dogs before she met me, even as few after I lived there...But I am granny's most special girl@ I am living my best life. I have many human, cat, even dog friends. I am friendly, affectionate, and gentle. I am not lonely or afraid anymore. I got for lots of car rides, big adventures. I am happy saved me, but granny says I saved her... xoxox


Love,

Charlotte

# A Prayer From Tucker
### For: Angie Pizelo

Dear Heavenly Dog Father,

I know that all dogs are life forms of God. I accept for myself, Tucker, the divine perfection of God. Every cell in my body radiates the healing love energy of God. Every organ of mine functions perfectly. I am experiencing, within my soul, the enthusiasm of exploration of the world of form and the wonderment of human friendship. This I know to be the truth of my beingness now, and I release this into the law of the Universe with gratitude, knowing that it is so, and so it is.

Love Your Doggie,

Tucker

# Eternity

### For: Rosemary Carl

Dear Heavenly Dog Father,

You have blessed me with a good home and a person who loves, adores, and cherishes me. I pray that you give all dogs a life like mine since all dogs are sweet, innocent souls who deserve the best in life. And when it's time for us to leave this world, please grant us all a quiet exit that's as painless as possible for our trip to heaven. There we will wait patiently for the people we love to join us for all eternity. Amen.

Love,

Betsy

# Our Furry Family
### For: Vanessa Schön

Dear Heavenly Dog Father This Is For My Mom,

Dear Mom,

I was the first you rescued.

You saw me on the street and gave me a home.

Then my first sister came along. She was hit by a car and abandoned before coming home.

After that, Kinsley joined us. She was also hit by a car and thankfully survived.

Then it was five of us, when you brought Sophie home. She was left in a box on the road.

Mom, thanks for giving us all a home. I am slightly annoyed to have to share my treats and toys, but I thank you for giving us all a family!

Love,

Winston

# We Will Be Reunited Once Again

### For: Joanne Ocasio
### Roxy 3 November 2007 - 20 August 2020

Dear Heavenly Dog Father,

On Christmas Day 2007, Roxy came into our lives I wanted her for my daughter who was 4. Roxy had all kinds of nicknames, but one that stuck with her until the end was wiggle butt because when she was excited her whole back end would shake. When we got Roxy, we had two Jack Russells Lucy and Charlie. When Lucy and Charlie passed away Roxy was an only fur child and she was sad she was missing something so we decided we needed a new baby in the family so we adopted Marcy in 2015, Roxy was 8 years old, and I wasn't sure how she would be with Marcy who was only 6 weeks old. Boy, were we surprised Roxy took to Marcy as if she was Marcy's mother? The bond was beyond anything we could have imagine it was beautiful. I had never seen such a bond between two dogs with such a big age difference. Marcy's love for Roxy was beautiful they were best friends. Roxy's passing took a toll on my baby Marcy she went into deep depression it's only now after several months that she is finally coming around to her old self. There are still times that Marcy gets up in the middle of the night to go search for her best friend. This picture is the love they had for each other. Marcy did not go a day without giving her big sister kisses. Roxy will be forever in our hearts.

To my beloved Roxy, you left me in August after I left for work, I think you did that on purpose as you always did things your way. You were my wiggle butt my silly boxer

girl that gave us 12 1/2 years of laughs, and cries that I will treasure for the rest of my life. Your little sister Marcy misses you so much. One day we will all be reunited again I truly believe this.

Love,

Your mommy and daddy and the rest of our pack.

PS. Can you add this for my friend Barb Furano, she just lost her little brown girl Mya?

Our little Brown Girl Mya you touch us all through your mom (Barb) you are a special little girl that your mom rescued but, you truly rescued her and will be forever in our hearts. (In loving memory of Mya)

# Thank You For Saving Our Lives.
### For: Essie Rheaume

Dear Heavenly Dog Father,

Thank you for giving me such wonderful humans to take care of me. I knew the minute I saw my mom that she was the one you chose for me. She even picked out a great dad to love me like she does. They give me tasty food to eat and a nice warm bed to sleep in at night. They even brought home a little brother, whom they call Henley, to play with me even though I was unsure I liked him. Now he's my best friend. Before my mom came along, I was scared and unsure about life. The humans before gave up on me and took me to a place called the shelter for dogs with no homes. I had no idea what I had done to deserve this in life. But now I understand it was part of your greater plan for me. You gave me the best humans possible. They make me feel safe and warm. In return, I give them lots of kisses and protect them from harm. I'm praying that all animals in the shelter are given a wonderful family like mine.

Amen,

Rugby & Henley Rheaume

# My Mom
### For: Kelly Chaffee

Dear Heavenly Dog Father,

I know this prayer is a little different from my normal prayers. I am usually praying that my mom does not catch me getting into the cat food. I also often pray that my mom will clean my pee up off the new hardwood floors before my dad sees it. I'm unsure why he gets so angry about that. After all, I am only marking my territory so no one else can take my mom. Doesn't he understand anything? As I stated though, this prayer is different. I am praying to you that my mom will be able to get through it if something happens to one of my siblings, and I have a lot of them! My blood brother (Tadies) and I are both 16 and every night I hear her thank God that we were healthy, safe, and happy that day and that we will stay healthy, safe, and happy tomorrow and for many years to come. I pretend that I'm sleeping but she will kiss me and say I love you so much Bellsi. Yes, mom, I know you do. Some days Tadies and I will run and play just to hear her say "oh look at my puppies". (The things we do for humans....) A few days ago, a cat sibling named Sumi became ill and had to go to the vet. I usually only pay attention to what pertains to me, but I heard my mom praying for Sumi too. My mom hardly ate for several days also. I know this for a fact because I usually try to steal her food when she's not looking. She was so upset....over a dang cat!!! Can you believe it? Sumi is back from the vet and feeling better which, I have mixed feelings over, as with him eating, there is less food to steal. Yet I guess I'm happy if my mom is happy about it.So heavenly father, PLEASE help my mom find the strength to get through the day if anything happens to one of my siblings. As for me? NO WORRIES....I'm going to live forever! I heard my mom say that one day after she got done listening to a song called "Only the Good Die Young

Love,

Bellsi

# AJ My Love
### For: Denise Kenitzer

Dear Heavenly Dog Father,

Please Heavenly Dog Father watch over my Mommy & my girlfriend (Toto) who will sorely miss me when I am gone. I have been her emotional support for the last 13 years. And am truly hoping & praying that I can be with her for a long, long time.

AJ came to me at a time he needed me & I needed him. I thank you & AJ for that. Please Heavenly Dog Father we need your strength to get through all this heartache. I lay here & watch you sleep as you take every breath, I feel as if my heart is being torn from my chest.

Many have come & gone before you. Not sure why this one seems so different. You are my heart AJ. I am going to be truly lost when you go. We are also praying for all those that have fur babies that have been lost or going through life ending times.

Please Heavenly Dog Father, help them to heal & let them know we will meet again. Please Heavenly Dog Father, give my family the strength they need to get through this. I would love to stay forever, but we both know that is not possible.

And most of all I want to say THANK YOU AJ for all the times you made me smile. The times you spent trying to cover & hide your food & beg for treats, you were definitely a food junkie. Mommy tried to do right by you. Thank you, Heavenly Dog Father, for all those fur babies that you have brought into our lives.

Sincerely,

  AJ & Mommy (Denise)

# Lots Of Prayers For The Best Dad Ever
### For: Matt DeMeyer

Dear Heavenly Dog Father,

My prayer is for daddy to recover quickly from his neck and spinal surgery so he can walk me again like he used to. Dear Heavenly Dog Father, please I beg of you. I don't want dad to be stuck forever using a walker or crutches. He is the best daddy a rescue puppy could ever ask for. I used to be in a kennel on death row with just one week left to live. I felt locked in a prison. Now look where I am today. I am surrounded by my daddy's love. Long ago he saved me. He says now it is up to me to save him. And Heavenly Dog Father with your help I will.

Love your girl,

Jenny

# Be With My Mommy

### For: Melinda Stanberry Austin

Dear Heavenly Dog Father, be with my Mommy

She does so much for me

She puts me above everything else

She loves me unconditionally.

Dear Heavenly Dog Father, be with my Mommy

She does her very best

If I am not feeling well

My Mommy does not rest.

She wakes me in the morning

With loving smiles and kisses

Then helps me down off the bed

So, I can go do my business.

She walks with me around the yard

And sometimes I have to stop and rest

But God my Mommy sits down beside me

Because she knows I'm doing my best.

Dear Heavenly Dog Father, be with my Mommy

She has so much to do

But she always loves and comforts me

No matter what she's going through.

Dear Heavenly Dog Father, be with my Mommy

She's watched my face grow gray

But her love for me grows stronger

Each and every day.

Dear Heavenly Dog Father, be with my Mommy

I'm the apple of her eye

No matter what life has thrown her way

She has never left my side.

Dear Heavenly Dog Father, be with my Mommy

I've shared her many tears

I hear her pray for me each day

That we remain together

For many, many more years.

Love,

 Moette

# A Simple Prayer For Dogs
### For: Carmelo Abela

Dear Heavenly Dog Father,

I pray that people won't hurt dogs anymore I can't understand why they leave them behind. I wish people had more feelings and understand them more. That is my only prayer and I ask in earnest.

Love,

Tina

# Momma Needs A Helping Hand

### For: Debbie Pack

Dear Heavenly Dog Father,

It is me again Stanley.

I know I just talked to you yesterday and the day before and the day before that, but I really wanted to talk to you today because I think my Momma is in need of you right now.

She is chasing Molly all over the house, trying to get the leash on her but Molly is darting in and out of the rooms. When Momma went to go in the bedroom, Charlie shut the door right in her face with his front paws. Momma didn't look too pleased, and I heard her say over and over "LORD HELP ME FOR I AM ABOUT TO LOSE MY MIND."

Could you please send down a helping hand for Momma or maybe a dog biscuit or two for me cause I am being good.

Thank you, tell my brothers and sisters hi for me and I will talk to you tomorrow.

Amen

Stanley

# Hopes Prayer
### For: Colette Patnaude

Dear Heavenly Dog Father,

My name is Hope, I want to pray for my momma you see she's very brave she's been fighting TNBC for almost 5 years. Heavenly Dog Father please watch over her. You see I need my momma and she needs me, she's a great mom she's funny and kind we love our snuggles, I would like her to stay around longer. I know she can't live forever but Heavenly Dog Father please give her the strength I'll give her the kiss and love she needs amen.

Thank you, Heavenly Dog Father,

Love,

Hope

# The Defenseless
### For: Henry M, Pitbull Matimos

Dear Heavenly Dog Father.

Almighty God l ask you for All the animals on earth, for each defenseless little animals, that you protect them from All the mistreatment and abuse of the human beings. Because they are your creation even the wildlife in Africa. Please keep them, each of one of them, from everything bad. Even Scooby and Tyson.

Amen Heavenly Dog Father.

Love,

Tyson, Scooby, and Hunter (in heaven)

# Hold Mine Until I Am Called

### For: James Demos

Our Heavenly Dog Father,

Now that my time with my sweet canine companion has passed, I pray you take my dear Jammies, and all the rest of my departed pack to watch over. I pray you dispatch your mighty Angels to carry her to your loving arms and keep her safe at the Rainbow Bridge until I myself am called home.

Amen.

Love Jammies

# One Day We Will Be Together Again
### For: Toni And Kevin Siddle

To The Heavenly Dog Father,

We are fur babies of Toni and Kevin Siddle (mum and dad to us!)

We miss them so much; we know mum says a little rhyme before she goes to sleep every night about us.

We know they miss us all so much as we miss them too, but we know one day we will all be together again. We can't wait for that day to come so we can cover them with licks and love

This is from our 4 muskahounds,

Jet, Snoop, Billy and Cider

X X X X

# Perfect Love Does Indeed Transform Every Fear Into Joy And Happiness

From: Suzanne Carter, MA, LPC, Unity Minister & Spiritual Director

To My Dear Heavenly Dog-Father,

I thank you so much for helping me have some Golden Retriever in my wonderful breed-mix of Pyrenees, Newfoundland and Rottweiler. For this is how my Mommy found me at the Golden Retriever Rescue of the Rockies, aka as GRRR. I needed her and she needed me. I was homeless in Tulsa and I was so thin, I may not have made it much longer. But then you guided me to be found so I would travel to Colorado and be fostered at GRRR.

We have shared a most perfect love, and thank you too for letting her adopt me on 02-02-2020; a most magical day indeed.

She was there for me in every way helping me get over my PTSD, that is what she called It. All that I know is that I was very afraid of almost everything. But she never got mad at me, not even once when I was afraid or had accidents until my tummy got well. Thank you for helping her help me learn to go outside by myself, even though it took 6 weeks of us going out together in massive amounts of snow every time I went outside. And now because of your perfect love that moves through her to me, I am one of the bravest dogs around. I have very little fear now.

So, in our perfect love, this love that she sings about everyday telling me: "I love you more today than yesterday, but not as much as tomorrow," I have one request. May she

know how wonderful she is and may we have great success in our work as co-therapists. Thank you for helping me become her co-therapist as a certified therapy dog to help her with her foster kid clients.

I do have one more request. May all doggies in the entire world have parents like my Mommy so that all doggies can do the most important thing they do: CREATE LOVE SO THAT ALL BEINGS LEARN TO LOVE LIKE WE DOGS DO WHEN WE ARE LOVED SO PERFECTLY.

Thank you, my Heavenly Dog-Father, I love you so much and celebrate your love that moves through all creatures when they can have their fear transformed by love.

Love,

Romeo

Suzanne Carter

# Oscar Reaches Out From Heaven
**For: Pam Chastain**

Dear Heavenly Dog Father,

This is Oscar, you remember, I met you last Friday. My legs didn't work when I lived with my mom but now that I'm here with you, I can run, and jump and - watch me get the zoomies!!! I'm super-fast again and I don't hurt anymore, just like my mom told me I wouldn't. Speaking of my mom, she seemed really sad when she brought me to Dr. Sara's. She kept telling me I was going to be strong again and be able to run and not hurt anymore and that she loved me sooooo much, but I was sad hearing her cry. Heavenly Dog Father, I'm so happy now, I'm here with my grandpa, Winston and all of the other dogs and cats and birds and gerbils and hamsters - even baby bunnies my mom took care of. But I want my mom to be happy too. Heavenly Dog Father, I know you've done so much for me already, but may I ask you to please help my mom be happy again? She loved me so much! She rescued me, she let me sleep on her bed with her and when I had bad dreams, she was always there to comfort me. She rubbed my belly all of the time, massaged my back when I was hurting and was always there when I needed her like when it got to where I couldn't walk, and she held me lovingly so I could pretend I was doing it myself. I love her so much and I know she knew how much I loved her because I gave her kisses and snuggled her always. Dear Father, please let her smile again. Please let her fall asleep without tears falling down her cheeks. When she wakes up at night, please let her remember I'm not there and let her fall back to sleep, instead of looking where I slept, rubbing her hand

across my space on the bed and start crying. She was a super loving mom and I want her to be happy like she used to be. That's all. Thank you, Heavenly Dog Father, I love you. I'm going to go play with Winston now. Amen.

With all my love,

Oscar.

Oscar was quite a talker. If it's too much, let me know and I'll try to downsize. I picked up his ashes today. Gosh I miss him so much. But I am so very happy for him to be free of all that held him back.

Thank you. Please keep in touch. You seem to touch my heart knowing what I'm going through and what others are going through. You have helped a lot, Lara, and I'd like to be there if you ever need it, or if you know someone that needs extra words of kindness from someone that knows what they are going through. Thank you from my whole heart.

# **Annabelle's Prayer**
### For: Lynn Bihary

Dear Heavenly Dog Father,

I pray and ask you to watch over all fellow canines.

Please protect and guide them.

May good health and happiness be with them always.

May their food bowls, water bowls, and toy boxes always be filled.

May love and affection surround them.

Amen.

Love,

Annabelle

# A New Life

### For: Abdennabi Ferchichi

Dear Heavenly Dog Father,

We ask that you grant our wonderful master a new job and money. We have seen him worry at night about how he will pay his bills. We want him to find true love, a life filled with happiness and wonderful health. Heavenly Dog Father, as you already know we do our best to protect him and let him know he will be alright no matter what life brings. We love him to the moon and back.

Love,

Sado, Zar, Frido , Zika, and Warda.

# Dear Souls
### For: Ileana Stroe

Dear Heavenly Dog Father,

Good god, rest in peace the dear souls of my puppies in heaven. Ledy, Codita, Boschetel, Dely, Bursuc, Mocsy, Mity. And protect me Ileana and my dear Kitten Griuta to be healthy.

Amen

# My Restful Place xxx
## For: Steve and Sally Turner

Dear Heavenly Dog Father,

Well here I lie between my mum and dad ,no place I would rather be .They let me have the best place on their bed .I watch them sleep at night ,knowing how safe I will always be .Their gentle touches when I wake at night ,their kisses on my face .Long ago I was in a bad place but then my parents recused me .They brought me home to a place full of love ,where I am so adored. I even have a brother who adores me too. My older brother loves me and when my mum and dad go out he's always there for me .I think of all the other dogs who do not have a home ,I know my mum and dad get so sad when they read about them all alone .In a perfect world I would wish for every dog to have a home and a nice warm bed .I hope someday this will be true because we have such big hearts and so much love to give

By,

Jasper our darling little boy xxx

# Bad Ass Biker
## For: Charlie King

Dear Heavenly Dog Father

Please help my Mom. She has so much on her, but she always takes care of me. I'm not only her Hero, she's mine. Mommy didn't want a girl pup, she chose me above all the boys. We are so grateful for putting us together.

Amen

No. It's Bab's. (Bad ASS Biker) I'm just Mommy. Charli King to the rest of the world. Feel free to use my name.

# Hawwy's Prayer

**For: Harrilyn Noelani Kiyoko Samson**

**Animal rescue is my mission as a way to contribute to God's**

Dear Heavenly Dog Father,

I wuv Mamaz so much. She gibs me tweats, toyz, and spoilz me rotten wif hooman food: wike. Fanks 4 blessing mez wif her.

Love, Puppy kisses & piggy snorts

Harry

# The Unsinkable Molly Brown
### For: Cathi Harley

Dear Heavenly Dog Father,

There are not enough thank you's for me to give you for sending my mom to me. I had given up. I was in a concrete run with 3 other dogs, and we were supposed to be PTS (not sure what that means except those dogs went away and never came back).

I heard rumors about people like my mom during the 12 days I was in the concrete prison. "Rescuers" were the name the other dogs whispered late at night in prayers to you. She and my dad came to see me a warm August afternoon. My Mom had tears in her eyes when she saw me. I couldn't even bring myself to come to the front of the run where she waited for me. I was dirty, weak, and tired. She asked one of the volunteers to bring me to her. I wrapped myself around her neck begging her to never leave me. She held me close, we walked around the grass, she promised me she would come get me the next day…and SHE DID!

I have heard Mom tell the story of me getting my name "Molly" from the Unsinkable Molly Brown on the ship, the Titanic. You see, heavenly father, that someone messed up my paperwork at the shelter. I was marked PTS for 8/12. My Mom didn't come to the shelter until 8/13. The mean woman at the front office told my mom "She was either PTS last night or she may be in Run 525 in Building 5." Lucky for me, I was still in the run. I was unsinkable!

I went to live with Mom, Dad and Misty. I loved Misty

but the feeling was not mutual right away. I arrived on a Friday and Misty ignored me for 3 days. I went to Mom's vet that Monday for something called a "well puppy check". We were gone longer than anyone wanted to be, and Misty was SO HAPPY to see me when we got back, and we were best friends until she passed away. I miss her silly wave she would do when Mom or Dad came home.

After we moved to Oregon, we got Max. She was my size when we first rescued her, but she is now SO BIG! I am still the boss and tell her every day. Heavenly father, I love my mom and Dad so much. They take good care of me and Max. Mom feeds us, does our hair, and nails, buys us lovies to play with, gives us super comfy beds to relax in, takes us to the park every day and on road trips every chance we get. Dad gives us baths and plays with us every day. We sleep with them at night even though Dad snores!

I am now 14 years old and know my years with Mom won't be that many more. I will one day cross over the Rainbow Bridge and see all the dogs Mom and Dad have rescued over the years. I will tell them that she continues to take care of the dogs and cats just like when they were there with her.

Love,

The "Unsinkable Molly Brown" Molly

# Some Joy Coming From Sadness
### For: Melanie Llewellyn

Dear Heavenly Dog Father,

My mammy, the day you picked me up I knew how much you needed me, I snuggled up on your lap for the 2 hour car journey to my forever home, I loved you so much and I knew how much you loved me, you told me every day, I didn't want to leave you, I stayed as long as I could, but I could see how heartbroken you were so that's why I sent you Daisy, I love you mammy.

Your Henry xx.

# Thank You, Lord, From a Rescue
## For: Scott McMichael

Dear Heavenly Dog Father,

Thank You, Lord, for caring for me,

my brothers and sisters, and my mom. You see

We were rescued from a horrible fate to be

Slated for "bait dogs" when we were just wee

You sent a hero who rescued us all,

just in time to be saved from our dreadful fall

We went far away,

to a place in Pennsylvania (MAJR inc.)

specially for Jack Russell Terrier rescues, as I recall

Thank You for caring, but wait, best of all

Lord, You saved us, Your love did surround

They found us loving homes where love abounds

My family loves me and treats me so well,

Thanks for reaching out to us, in that place that was hell.

From: Bandit (alias Abilene)

Special thanks to: Mid- Atlantic Jack Russell rescue - MAJR Inc. / www.majr.org

# Michelle's Dog Bears Prayer
### For: Michelle Inabinett

Dear Heavenly Dog Father

It's Bear Here!!!

I want to thank You for giving me the best mom in the World.

I had several families before You gave me a super Mom like Michele. Nobody ever showed me the love that she showed me. I knew she lived across the street, and I knew her husband was sick and needed my help. I tried to show her how good I could be.  She was always having to take her husband to the doctor, but she found ways to always show me her love, and I wanted to show it back.

Dog Father, I wish I had more than four years to help her through such a rough time.  At least I could be there when her husband passed!  She needed my protection, because she was now alone. Please help her new dog, Dax, protect her, and if You will allow me to go back on earth, I'd Love to have her as my Mom. She was the best!

All My Respect

Bear

# Mummy Marion and Special Friend Ashley

**For: Ashley Halloween**

Dear Heavenly Dog Father,

My mummy took me in when I was abandoned.

She took me home and called me "Star."

She loved me more every day.

She walked with me, talked with me, played with me.

She's been there through good times and bad.

She's my "Star,"

And when two Stars meet, the whole world lights up.

My special mummy is forever and always.

Love,

Star

# We Are So Thankful
### For: Jean Davis

Dear Heavenly Dog Father,

My name is Snowy, and my mom's other little doggie is named Barbie. My mom named me Snowy because I am so white. My mom told the lady she got Barbie from that she was trying to figure out what to name her. And the lady said her mother passed away on the day the puppies were born. They were a week early, and she felt like her mother sent the puppies early so she would have something to keep her busy. She suggested the name Barbie because her mother's name was Barbara. Well, that's my first name, so she had to be named Barbie. Barbie and I have a fenced in back yard to play and run to get our exercise. We just love living here with our mom.

Signed,

Snowy and Barbie

# Eternal Kingdom
### For: George Noujaim

Dear Heavenly Dog Father,

I ask You to welcome the earthly dogs who are no longer with us into Your heavenly Garden of Eden where there is no pain. Glory to You, oh Heavenly Dog Father!

Love.

Sam

# Loving My Mom
### For: Debbie Kaufman

Dear Heavenly Dog Father,

I'm coming to You to ask You to please let my mom know how much I loved and miss her. She was so kind to me through all the years. When she would wake up, I would kiss her first thing. When she went to work, I lay by the door for her to return. Others could come thru that door, but I waited on her. Once she was home, I was her shadow, even at times stepping on the back of her shoes to where she would almost fall. She never yelled at me, but just would pet me. I loved her so. I am no longer with her, but could You please comfort her?

Sincerely,

Annie,

AKA the best blue heeler ever

# Fresh Start!
## For: James Dovel

Dear Heavenly Dog Father!

Well, that was a wild ride of a life! Mom and Dad knew I was sick when the rescue group delivered me. I was all ready to come back to the Rainbow Bridge very quickly. My birth mom had noninfectious mange. What chance did I have? I was only four weeks old. I still remember the look my Dad, Jim, gave me, and the words he said: "Now we have our work cut out for us. He was right, because the regular vet was lost on what treatments she thought would work. Most puppies that have mange don't make it. Usually, they are sent back to You, Dog Father, for a new start. I was lucky, and my Mom and Dad caring enough, that I had a chance to live. Well, it was too short, but my Mom and Dad took me all over the country when they traveled. In my eleven years, I got to visit more places and meet more friends than most Dogs do. Thank You, Heavenly Dog Father, for my Mom and Dad and all the fun I had. I know my parents were really upset that I crossed the Rainbow Bridge before their trip, but I'm watching this trip from heaven, and it's for the best!

Your girl,

Raven

# Rescue's
### For: Kaitlyn Harrison

Dear Heavenly Dog Father,

Of all the misplaced broken spirits,

I may not be the most well trained

Of all the personalities.

Mine may not be the most outgoing,

But You took a chance on me

So I took a chance on You!

Skittish became mischievous

Then shifted to amusing,

Converting into affection,

Transforming into loyalty.

The fondness that I feel for You

Will never fade away.

Thank You for loving me

For the remainder of my days.

Love,

-Blue and Pepper

# **Prayers For Gemma**
## For: Elizabeth Stetler and Gemma

Dear Heavenly Dog Father,

As I sit here this evening, I am praying for You to please take care of Gemma there in Heaven, at the Rainbow Bridge. She passed away a year ago on the 29th of June, and I still remember holding her so dear, so close, with tears streaming down my face, and feeling as though my world had shattered. I sit here with a candle lit in her memory and honor and her ashes close by. She brought me so much joy, and always wanted to snuggle her muzzle in close and fall asleep with her head on my shoulder. I am in tears, as my shoulder is now empty and bare. I long for her fur to nestle against my neck and feel her breathing once again. I pray that she is no longer in pain and able to play with no limitations, and that she will remember me that one great day when we can all be reunited. While my heart is still broken, I still have her sister, Bonnie, with me. She is getting older, has many medical concerns, and is almost 10 years old. I pray that You and Your angels surround her with healing love, and that Bonnie is able to enjoy her life here on earth before joining her sister Gemma in Heaven and the Rainbow Bridge. I am not ready to let her go yet, as I just lost Gemma a year ago. I pray these things as the candle burns bright and the stars are shining outside my bedroom window. I can see the wind blow through the trees, and I can feel a sense of peace as I say this prayer. I cannot thank You enough for all that You have given me and the love that You have allowed Gemma and Bonnie to share with me. I rescued them years ago, but in the end, they were the ones who rescued me. I end this prayer tonight with a wish that Gemma is happy tonight, cuddling somewhere warm, and happy once again. Sleep, sweet precious Gemma, wherever you may be, and I send you all my love. And with that, I will pull down the shade, blow out the candle, and say goodnight.

Thank You, Heavenly Dog Father, and Good Night. Amen.

Love, Elizabeth Stetler

# I Am Furever Grateful By Sykes Morton
### For: Lauren Morton

Dear Heavenly Dog Father,

When I wake up in the morning, the first thing, I do is say a thank You prayer for all the blessings You have bestowed upon me. I thank You for giving me my human parents who have provided a life for me like none other! I am so thankful that they have provided me with shelter from the elements as we live in hot florida. I am so very thankful for the king size bed we sleep in every nite (larger would be nice, though). Thank you also for making sure i have that handy dandy doggie door to go in and out of about 100 times every day. It has uncomplicated my life from having to come to the humans to let me out. Thank you, also, for the millions of lizards that live in my back yard and provide me with hours of entertainment.

Watch over my parents so they can continue to care for me. Watch over their hands so meat and cheese roll ups can still be made for me.

I am especially thankful that my parents never tire from playing endless hours of throw the ball. Please see that their arms do not fail them! I love my sister allie, but she can't throw a ball. Allie is a definite step up from the lizards!

And, yes, I am so grateful that my human parents saw that I needed a playmate and got me a sister to torment day and night.

I thank You for my parents' ability to swim and play doggie in the middle with me, even though I should be training

for the summer olympics! Who knew i would be such an accomplished swimmer?

I have countless reasons to be grateful and thankful, but honestly it really boils down to having the absolutely best human parents in the world. They have made me their world, and I never take them for granted.

I have to go now. Dad is revving up the truck, and I so love to stick my head out and bark at passersby, so I will close by saying thank You, Heavenly Dog Ffather, for all the blessing You have given me in this life!

Woof and amen,

Sykes

# My Best Friend

### Judy Weiss, Founder of Happiestdogsever.com

Dear Heavenly Dog Father,

I want to give love and so much thanks to Judy, my guardian and best friend in the whole world! From the first day she brought me home from my breeder, we became best friends. Every day since then, she seems to spend every waking moment making sure I am happy and healthy. She takes such good care of me, always ensuring that I eat only healthy food with just the right calories, playing with me every day, and most importantly, giving me belly rubs on demand!

Because of her, I am a super-healthy 15-year-old dog, always happy and always loved! Can You believe I still do Zoomies around the house? Mom loves when I do that!

Judy has always allowed me to lounge on my favorite spot in the house, the armchair in the living room. From that vantage point, I can keep an eye on Judy just so I know where she is at all times. And if she goes upstairs for a while, I, of course, head up there just to check on her.

Every morning, I wake up and can't wait to spend my day with my best friend, Judy!

Love,

Roxy, Mini Poodle

Wishing you continued success with doing what you do to help 100 dogs!

# Gone Too Soon!
## For: Lori

Dear Heavenly Dog Father,

This is Your little girl, Molly.

I have a real dilemma on my hands. My Mom is just so sad that I was called home to You so soon, but for the first time in over a year I am free from pain. I know You've heard my Mom's prayers. She and my Dad loved me so much.

I know they and the vets did their best to make me feel better. I hope there are a lot of toys to play with in heaven. My trip over the Rainbow Bridge was so peaceful. Being such a little girl, I was afraid when I got to the bridge. You sent me a new friend named Bear. He made me so much less afraid that no other dogs try to mess with me. Everybody has been so nice here. Please tell my Mom and Dad that I am free from pain and can now play with all the other dogs here in heaven.

Your little girl,

Molly

# Just One More Day
## For: Lyn Konopacky

Dear Heavenly Dog Father,

I need to talk to You about my mom. You see, she is really worried about me. I hear her talking to You about me.

I hear her say, "thank You for another day with my baby. Please heal him. Give me just one more day to love him."

She tells everyone that I am her miracle baby. She says that I am alive because of You. She knows you will want me back someday, but she hopes it isn't soon. I am sad because she is sad. Father, let me stay a little longer. I promise I will be good. I will try to eat my supper like a good boy. I won't cry if she gets the needle in wrong.

You see, God, I love my mom and she needs me. I know she is trying to help me. Bless my Mom and please let me stay one more day. Thank You, Heavenly Dog Father.

One more thing, Heavenly Dog Father. I know this is hard for me, but I promise I will try really hard not to pee all over the floor.

Amen,

Rexy

# Hold Mine Until I Am Called
**For: James Demos**

Our Heavenly Dog Father,

Now that my time with my sweet canine companion has passed, I pray You take my dear Jammies and all the rest of my departed pack to watch over. I pray You dispatch Your mighty Angels to carry her to Your loving arms and keep her safe at the Rainbow Bridge until I, myself, am called home.

Amen.

Jammies

# My Marley
### For: Pam Stout

Dear Heavenly Dog Father,

I want to thank You for giving me my mom, who is also my best friend. I love her so much and I know she loves me too. No matter what time I have to go outside, she will get up to let me out. We share a special bond, made stronger because I have epilepsy and she always helps me through this. I know I can be a butthead, but she still loves me unconditionally. I cannot believe how lucky we were to find each other. I needed a new home and she had been looking all over for me. Thank goodness we found each other! Heavenly Dog Father, thank You so much for helping my mom find me. It is the greatest gift of all!

Love,

Pam Stout, owned by Marley

# A Prayer of Thankfulness
## For: B'nai Madden

Dear Heavenly Dog Father,

This is Snoopy and Bear. Just wanna say thank You for our furever home. We have a great family. It gets a little crazy at times, but we're happy. They keep us fed and full of treats. But we're praying for our mommy, who hasn't been feeling well lately. Please help make her better so she can continue to take care of us.

Thank You!

Snoop and Bear

# Rescued Hearts
# (since we rescued each other)
## To: Velvet Urgo

Dear Heavenly Dog Father,

I want to take a minute, not to ask for anything from You but to simply say thank You for all that I have.

I am thankful for my wonderful new family. They care for me, love me, give me lots of belly rubs, snugglins, take me for walkies, bye-bye rides in the car, give me treaties (my favorites are the non-rawhide bones). I love to hear the story about how I was rescued and my life changed for the better four years ago when they saved me.

I showed up at their house one day, and my Momma said she fell in love with me at first sight. My long, basset hound ears were flapping in the breeze as my short legs moved me through the field fast. I stopped by daily for food, water, and treats and eventually started sleeping on their porch. My then non-fur brother saw me shivering and got me a nice doghouse with my name on it to sleep in. One day I disappeared. My momma made some phone calls and found I had been picked up from animal control. They said I had been there 5 days and was available to be adopted. The next day I was rescued. I was so happy to be out of doggie jail! I got a nice baffie and a new collar. I was so happy to have a warm house and nice doggy bed to sleep in. It surely was an adjustment for me, but my new family was very patient. I was so afraid of everyone and everything, due to my past. I had to learn there were rules staying inside--I wasn't supposed to chase the cats and had to go outside to potty. I'm a pretty smart guy and caught on quickly. I am still scared when meeting new people but warm up to them as soon as I figure out that they can be trusted. My momma often wonders who rescued whom? We are all so thankful and blessed to have one another! Everything happens for a reason. God sent me to them, and I am the happiest boy ever!!

Love, Droopy

# Koda's Story

### For: Pamela Anne Stout

Dear Heavenly Dog Father,

I am writing to You because You led me to find a special person to take care of me. You see, I had a horrible relationship with humans before my mom came to get me. I am terrified of men with hats or hoodies on, and brooms make me shake in fear. To say I was mistreated is an understatement. But You still helped me find a mom with enough patience and love, so I was finally able to relax. I now have a dog brother that is horribly spoiled, but my mom makes sure I am spoiled too. I am still afraid of men--I guess that will never go away--but now I have a family to protect, and I am extremely protective of them. So, thank You, Heavenly Dog Father, for giving me a family that loves me and I love them.

Love,

Pam Stout, owned by Koda and Marley

# Rose
### For: Dale Cherry

Dear Heavenly Dog Father,

Thank You so much for the gift You gave me when my Ruby passed away. A customer I was doing tree work for gave me his dog. Her name is Rose. What a gift that a stranger would do that!! The only thing I know is that You stepped in my life at that time when You knew my heart was broken. Now that she has passed, my heart is broken again. But, Heavenly Dog Father, I know that one day we will be together again. Me and my Rose.

Amen.

'Rose'

# My Mommy's Heart
### For: Chris Hughes

Dear Heavenly Dog Father,

My name is Ginger. I started life as an unwanted puppy. I was thrown away when the people I lived with got a divorce. So, I went out with the trash. I was so sad. I spent my days in a cage all by myself. I would pray and pray for someone to come along and love me. All I wanted was a lap to sit in, a toy to play with, and a loving hand to scratch my back. And then, my miracle happened. A lady with a big heart took me in. She said I looked the color of ginger, so that is what she named me. She told me, "Here is your lap to sit on," as she lifted me onto hers. Then she handed me a toy. Here is a toy for you to play with. And she lovingly scratched my back. I soon had others to play with, as she filled our home with other puppies who needed a home full of love. You see, my Mommy has a big heart. But now, God, my Mommy needs Your help. Her heart has a problem, and she needs Your help. Dear God, please help her as she helped me. I love her so.

Thank You, dear Heavenly Dog Father.

Ginger

# An Umbrella of Protection
### For Daddy

Dear Heavenly Dog Father,

It's Peggy Sue Kantner. I just wanted to ask You to keep my dad and me under Your umbrella of protection. Heavenly Dog Father, as You can see from above, dad is a little stressed out worrying about health and finances. Dad can sometimes be a little grumpy and I worry about him. Can You also keep an eye on him too,?

Thanks for listening.

Love,

 Peggy Sue

# Till We Meet Again
### For: Dale Cherry

Dear Heavenly Dog Father,

I know my time has come. I am tired and weak. I know you will be waiting for me at heaven's gates with all my brothers and sisters. I will miss my family, but I know we will meet again.

We will all be young, and we can play all day long and be together forever. And, Heavenly Dog Father, let my family know that I am fine and free of pain and not to worry about me. One day we will meet again.

Amen

Rose

# Star's Prayer
### For: Marion Wadsworth

Dear Heavenly Dog Father,

I thank my mummy for each day

For giving me love and a place to stay.

I had no home and was on the streets,

Then a rescue found me for people to greet.

A lady came to see me. I loved her from the start, and I prayed that she would take me home and love me with all her heart.

She did that was when I was just a puppy.

I'm now 15 years old, and my love for my mummy is endless.

Thank you, Mummy for each day,

For my lovely warm bed and toys to play

For our walks and our cuddles are far from few. God Bless you, Mummy,

I love you forever.

Star

# Babs Prayer
### For: Charli King

Dear Heavenly Dog Father,

Please take care of my Mom. She rescued me when everyone ignored me. I played in her Hospital bed and kissed her.

Love,

Babs

My LOL Bab's saved me.

# Sweetness Alert
## For: Bill Lawton

Dear Heavenly Dog Father,

Thank You for blessing me with a family that saw the potential in me, loves me, cares for me, provides a safe and warm home to sleep in, and makes sure I get lots of toys, exercise, and treats when I do well with my training. If I had all the power in the world, I would have my biological mom and eight brothers and sisters join me. I know they would love my new Mom and Dad as much as I do.

In Your name, Amen.

Zack

# A Dogs Dream

### For: Alyssa Ferraro -Happy Jacks

Dear Heavenly Dog Father,

I pray that every dog will feel the unconditional love I feel for my own

I pray that each hound will always feel joy and be safe and sound

I pray for a world where every stray will have a comfy place to lay

I pray that every human will see that dogs are so special and to our hearts, they hold the key

I pray that every pup all around the world will feel love because that is all they truly deserve

I pray no dog is ever alone and that each one finds its perfect home

Amen,

Cookie

# Roxie's Prayer
## For: Leslie Roberson

Dear Heavenly Dog Father,

Thank You for the warm bed, plenty of good food, and humans who love me. But do You think You could do something about that leash when I'm trying to catch a rabbit?

From,

Roxie, the rescue Jack Russell.

## To My Toupee

I always knew the day would come
We'd have to say goodbye
Though I've walked down this path before
I'm not prepared little girl of mine

When I'm happy or when I'm sad
You're always by my side
Your love is unconditional
Little girl of mine

I watch you breathing next to me
As I pray for another day
To love to laugh to run and play
Little girl of mine

When your human sister was a baby
I affectionately called her Toupee
That's how you got your name
Never to call out that name again
Is half driving me insane

Like her, you never show any fear
I know You're protecting me
Wish I could be brave like You and her
Little girls of mine

As I'm trying to prepare
For the day you're no longer here
I wish you could tell me what to do
As I wash away my tears

I know the day is coming
When I have to let you go
But how do I say goodbye again
Little girl of mine

In your tender soulful eyes
I also can see hers
You were her little puppy
Maybe to her you must return

I love you little girls of mine
And until again I hold you tight
I'll hold on to all the love we shared
Every day and every night
Author Julie Rashell Richmond

# Prayers from Gunner
## To: My Family

Dear Heavenly Dog Father,

How is my little sister dog, Sweeny, doing in heaven? I really miss her a lot. We were such good friends down here. We would always snuggle together on the couch and chase each other around in the yard. I hope she is getting the treats she always loved and not barking too much. She was a nervous nelly when she was here. Tell her I said "hi" and I will see her again someday when I get there.

Oh, and while I have Your attention, I need to send up a prayer for my brother dog, Murphy. He is getting old and a bit irritable lately. Sometimes when my parents have treats to give us, he wants to fight, and my dad has to break us up. What's up with that? I like to share. I don't know what he is thinking. I mean his teeth are falling out and I know his gums hurt, so maybe that's the problem. Please help him to feel better. I don't like to fight.

And for my humans, Mom and Dad. Help them with the health issues they are facing. They are very good to us. I hear some people say they spoil us. I don't know what that means, but they treat us like their children, so I don't mind. We are a happy family and I love them just as much as they love us.

Well, that's it for now, until next time...

Thanks for all You do for us, my Heavenly Dog Father.

Love,

Gunner, (Your faithful little Dachshund)

# **Puppy Dreams**
## For: The Harrison Family

Dear Heavenly Dog Father,

Now they lay me down to sleep

My fury paws tucked under me

Nuzzled next to those I love

I pray for another day

To play in the yard

And squeak my toys

For belly rubs

And good boy praise.

Thank You, Lord, for this family I was gifted

With loads of treats

And sloppy kisses

As I close my eyes

And drift to sleep

I now know how love can run so deep

Love,

 Willow

# Prince Kiddo's Love
## For: Lary Schuette and Susan Nelson

Dear Heavenly Dog Father,

Thank You for blessing me with a family that saw the potential in me, loved me, cared for me, and provided a safe and warm home for me to sleep in. They made sure I got lots of toys, exercise, and treats. They provided me with the wheelchair I needed to get around because I couldn't walk in my own. I got to go to work with them every day. I was never alone or scared. I loved my Mom and Dad and all my special needs brothers and sisters so much; I miss them and I know they miss me terribly. I know they would love to have me back with them, but it was my time to go to heaven to be the angel that watches over them. Please bless them and give them the peace of knowing that I'm happy and healthy now and running with the angels and always watching over them. I love them very much.

In Your name, Amen.

Prince Kiddo

# June's Prayer,
### For: Brooke Holder

Dear Heavenly Dog Father,

Thank You for my home and my fur brothers and sisters and thank You for my human mommy who loves me more than anything. Thanks for kisses every day and snuggles every night. But if You don't mind, I'd like to take exercise off my chore list completely. I hear it causes wrinkles, and I have enough of those.

Amen,

June

# Dad Needs Help.
## For: James A Vey

Oh Heavenly Dog Father,

It's Machiavelli again. I am speaking to You on behalf of Einstein, too. He and I really love our Dad a lot, but he needs help with time and flavor. He's late a lot with our daily walks and sometimes just puts us in the yard, which is simple for him, but he needs these walks just as much as we do. We have to keep his heart rate up and get his daily mile in. We would also appreciate it if You helped him understand that a dog's palate needs more flavors than what the dog food companies create, and we would prefer meals more like his, which is why we beg so much and turn our noses at the food he gives us.

Thank You ever so much, Your two faithful followers,

Mac and Ein.

# Hugs
### Elyce Bohne-Remmel

Dear God,

Hi this is Jessie BabyGirl Jane.

I wanted to thank You for helping me find my new Mom and Dad in 2017. I'm sorry for taking so long, but I've been super busy learning about my new life and family.

Mom and Dad are almost always with me, and we take great walks several times a day, but we never go out in the rain so I don't get scared. If they have to leave for an appointment, they always make sure I have a calming cookie, and if they're gone longer than one or two hours, they always have someone come in and check on me so I don't worry or get lonesome and anxious, it's wonderful!

My grand nephews, James and Alex, hang out with me; we play, they give me treats, and we watch TV together. While Mom and Dad are gone for a week, James and Alex are even sleeping all night with me in Mom's and Dad's bed, so I don't even get lonesome or scared.

Thank You, thank You! You couldn't have picked a more perfect family for me, filled with lots of Love and Fun.

It's a million times better than that place I was before, where I was treated awfully as a bait dog and other icky stuff.

My Mom says they are very blessed and fortunate to get me and make everything the best part of my life. I agree and thank You, again, for taking good care of me on my journey and helping lead me to my Mom and Dad!

I Love You God,

Always and Forever!

Jessie babygirl Jane Remmel

# Coopers Prayer

### For: Shannon Ficken

Dear Heavenly Dog Father,

Hi, it's me Cooper. I just wanted to say thank You. You see, I know it was You who saved me that day so long ago from going to the shelter.

I remember being picked up from my house and taken to my dad's son's house. We used to go visit them all the time, and I'd play with their doggo, Gus. But that day was different. I hadn't seen my dad for a couple of days, and then all these people I didn't know showed up at Gus's house. Some were crying, some were quiet, some were just sniffling. Gus's mom passed around lots of food, drinks, and Kleenex. Gus kept circling around me and kinda pushed me into his mom's arms. She took us outside and played and played with us for a long time. Then she sat down with Gus and me and said she had to talk to us. She asked Gus if he'd like a brother and she asked me if I'd like to move in with them. I got kinda mad and said "No"! I want my dad! But Gus's mom explained that my dad had passed and was with God now. I cried for a while, and Gus and his mom hugged me to make me feel better. Pretty soon, we went back in the house. As we came in, mom heard someone ask who was going to take Cooper--that's me! Everyone said I should go to the shelter. Gus aarroood really loudly, and his mom just looked at his dad and said "no way! I think Cooper belongs here"! Everybody was talking at once, and I had to stop the noise, so I said really loudly that I wanted to stay here! Everybody got quiet and then started laughing! I was at my new home. But God, I have to say thank You again for bringing me here. You see, my buddy Gus got sick, and I think You wanted me here so I could help take care of him. You knew Mom and Dad#2 were going to need me to lean on when the time came for Gus to crossover. But You weren't done with me were You, God? You knew we Aussies need a job! So You had Mom#2 bring Chukar and Yogi home. Boy, what a chore they were to raise! Puppies aren't easy, and

mom#2 needed my help herding and rounding up those little buggers. Please God, be sure and let Mom#2 know that I really wasn't trying to drown Chukar in the toilet. He just wanted a drink, and who would have guessed that a bulldog could drink out of the toilet too?

But as You know, Heavenly Dog Father, I was getting older and I tired easily. Mom#2, Dad#2, Chukar, and Yogi noticed and took more time with me. Yogi shared the tv remote and loaded my bed full of toys, and Chukar dropped his treats in my bed sometimes. And thank You, God, for the snowstorm that day. It surprised Mom#2 that I could get outside into the yard without help that day. I loved to play in the snow, catch snowflakes on my tongue, and make snow angels. But Mom#2 must have known what was happening. You must have whispered in her ear, because she ran in the house and got my favorite blanket. She picked me up and carried me up on the deck and she cradled me in her arms. She called Dad#2 at his work, and he rushed home. It was my perfect day to cross the bridge, surrounded by my pawrents and brothers.

So, thank You, Heavenly Dog Father, for a wonderful life, really two! Please help Mom#2 and Dad#2 with the puppers! They can be a handful. I left instructions with the boys to keep the pawrents on their toes but to always be kind, and if that doesn't work, to make them laugh.

So, thank You, Heavenly Dog Father,

Love,

Cooper

# **Bianca**

Our love, our joy, our happiness

  As a Puppy-

    Abandoned, lost, found, rescued, adopted

    In need of security, stability, reliability, kindness

      We are grateful we found you

Young and growing-

Excited, happy, energetic, protective, running, herding, jumping, following instincts

    Blue Heeler, loyal and true, fast, and exuberant

    We are amazed as you embrace life

Adult-

Dynamic personality, watching our home, welcoming friends, playing with toys

    Devouring treats, pleading for tidbits, licking and kissing, loving

    Swimming at the lake, running at the cabin and camp, chasing squirrels, rabbits, butterflies,

      Eager to please,

        Loving attention, loving family, loving tummy rubs

          We are proud of what you have become

Mature-

Playing ball, fetching, still swimming, running, playing, chasing everything,

    Waiting for family, waiting for treats, protective of family

      Slowing down, but just a little

        We are enjoying every precious minute

Dawn of life-

Slowing down now, still trying to chase squirrels, protective, wading

in lake, still loving balls,

    Now Cancer, coughing, labored breathing, so very sick

    Needing rest, taking medication, still loving treats, needing hugs, difficulty walking, falling,

    Thirsty, fighting sickness

    Waiting for family acceptance

    Waiting for family to let go      Prayers to Saint Francis

    Searching for strength

Celebration of Life-

  Remembering, crying, wistful of memories, emptiness in our hearts and home

  Learning to move on, stepping forward, praying, searching, wondering

    Believing in power of love and family, opening hearts,

    Realizing hope, recognizing her soul

    Will be, will remain, will carry on, will be welcomed to a peaceful existence in light

    Because she was part of our family

    We are at peace

Bianca,

  Our hearts, our life, our joy…

    Forever

-Lori Grundy

# Blessings And Bones Bring Happiness
## For: Wendy L Jones

Dear Heavenly Dog Father,

I will start my prayer

It will be for all dogs out there

Here there and everywhere

I send blessings from my heart

Also, will say we will never part with love

Even when the soul's leaving comes

To say goodbye on the island

Over the Rainbow Bridge

It's where we will meet again

The prayer is to share with all who wish

It is sent from the heart of Rottweilers, all hugs and a big sloppy kiss

Love,

Posi Traction- my youngest, her love and protection is how she shows her worth

Torrington Bearing -the momma to all, high spirited and mellow loves the world

Hydraulic Bearing- my rescue girl, full of dancing running and grateful

For Gem, the Rottweiler, who made me love the breed so much, I started with jasmine and still kept going.

# Buddy's Prayer
## For: LeAnn Fuller-Smith

Dear GOD,

Hi, this is Buddy, You know me. I'm a good boy, and my momma and daddy love me so much. They are so worried about me. As You know, my doctor found a mass inside of me and they are trying their best to get me better. I'm not feeling too bad, I just throw up here and there. I just want to ask You to help me get better, and if it is not in Your plan for me to get better and stay here with my four bubbas and my sissy, then I just ask You to please don't let me suffer. If that is Your plan, God, please don't let my momma and my daddy have too much heartache. I know everyone will miss me as I will miss all of them, but You know, if and when I cross that Rainbow Bridge, You let everyone know that is where I am and that I will be waiting for everyone and will need someone to lean on. I love You God, and I thank You for letting my Jordan find me on that New Year's Eve and for letting me be so loved and well taken care of all these years.

Your Pal,

Buddy Ro!

# My Precious Romanian Rescue
## For: Kath Bradbury

Dear Heavenly Dog Father,

Rosie here. Thank You for sending Monika in Romania to find me and take me in with my sister and brother. Monika was my first mummy who helped me get over my traumatic start in life and found me a new mummy, Kath, whom I love dearly in another land called England in the UK. I miss my country and my sister and brother who can't be with me. Thank You for my new home where I feel safe and loved. I try to be good for my mummy, but sometimes I'm too noisy and naughty, so I'd like to say "sorry, Mummy." I know my mummy loves me; she's always telling me, and the good Rosie outweighs the naughty Rosie.

Love,

Rosie

Thank you for allowing Rosie to be in your book

# A Cry For Help
### For: Leisa Tilley Grajek, K9 Guardians

Dear Heavenly Dog Father,

I have been chosen to be a K9 Guardian service dog. There is a disabled military veteran in need of my help. I've heard that 22 veterans commit suicide every day and that service dogs save lives. My heart is brave, my body is strong, and my mind is set on the task ahead. Please continue to strengthen me and give me wisdom that I may rise to the occasion and handle all that is ahead of me. May there be more like me to help the many voices I hear crying out in hopelessness.

In Jesus' name, Amen.

K9 Guardians Capt. Sven

# Our Evening Prayer
### For: Eddie Iliescu

Allow me, Dear Heavenly Dog Father, to conclude

Evening prayer as usual:

Good Heavenly Dog Father,

When You want

Call me to You,

Please take it

First on my dog,

Leaving me alive:

When he died, he would suffer

Watching my cross at the top.

And don't consider me mischievous,

But be as hard as I am,

Heavenly Dog Father, have mercy on me,

After giving her soul, one more day:

I mourn his death.

Luna and Lino

# Saving Each Other Terry The Terrier
## For: Viv Allen

A dog's prayer to the Heavenly Dog Father,

I came into your life when you were sad and at your lowest. I was also sad pacing the doggy jail that I had ended up in. I was confused as to why I was there, and you were recovering from major surgery and the recent loss of your own doggy to cancer. You needed to walk every day to make yourself strong again. It also helped you mentally. I became lost and was picked up by the dog warden. You also felt lost emotionally, as your recent surgery meant that you could never have a family of your own. You took me for long walks, along with some of my other scruffy inmates who had no problems finding new homes. I was left in doggy jail for five and half months. My behavior in the doggy jail came across as aggressive, but I just couldn't cope with the noise of the barking and being cooped up 22 or 23 hours a day. You took me out and showed me off, purposely walking me around shops. You told all the humans who stopped to talk to us that I needed a loving new home, and if they were interested, to come and visit me but to not judge me by my behavior in the doggy jail, where I just couldn't cope. You would walk me to the park and put your coat on the floor for me so I could rest. It made you happy to watch me sleep, as you knew how stressed I was in the doggy jail. You came to see me almost every day, even in the snow. Your previous doggy had also come from a doggy jail. You loved her so much that you didn't think it was possible to love another furry as much as you loved her. One day, you came to see me, and I wasn't there. You went to the reception desk to find out where I was, and the kind lady said I was next door being neutered. You panicked slightly and asked if I had been reserved and if that was that the reason why I was being neutered. Sadly that wasn't the case, and I was just next in the queue. So that was the day when you realized you'd fallen in love with me and I would become yours and Daddy's next rescue doggy. That week, you brought my new Daddy down to meet me. He loved me straight away. I mean, who wouldn't? You asked the staff if

you could reserve me, and they were so pleased for me. The next day you turned up with a bottle of shampoo because I was rather stinky! You gave me a lovely bath at the doggy jail and then popped me in your car. I remember your laughing at me as I rubbed my face in the lovely fluffy blanket on the back seat of your car. I was coming for a trial run to my new home with you, but we all knew instantly that I wouldn't be going back to doggy jail. That was it! I was home, and it felt good. You and Daddy were super happy again--life without a doggy just doesn't suit you two. You went back to the doggy jail and signed all the paperwork for me so that I was forever yours and Daddy's. That was thirteen years ago, the day you saved me and in turn, I saved you and Daddy.

Terry the terrier

# My Saviour
### For: Lee Rand

Dear Heavenly Dog Father,

Booms was my life saver, literally, when he was only a pup about 6 months old. We had our boiler fixed, but unfortunately it wasn't sealed properly, so we had carbon monoxide gas leaking out. My son, Booms brother, was only six at the time and I kept getting headaches and flu-like symptoms.

After being out of the house for a while, we'd feel better until we went home.

After a few days, we were getting worse, and I fell asleep. Boomer kept barking continuously, which worried our neighbors, who called the ambulance. We spent two days in the hospital with carbon monoxide poisoning. So, Heavenly Dog Father, if Boomer didn't bark, we wouldn't be here today.

Love,

Lee To Booms

# Lucky Me!
### For: Bill Lawton

Hello, Dear Heavenly Dog Father,

I stand before You as a true believer that, due to Your love and guidance, good things happen to dogs. I am blessed with a Mom, a Dad, three brothers, and one sister. One of those brothers came into our lives recently and was rescued out of a very bad beginning. He's a little feisty but a great guy, and we play a lot. Also, thank You for a loving home where I can sleep where I want, eat delicious food, drink lots of water, and run in the yard with Zack until we are very tired. This is truly a great life, and I am eternally grateful for being chosen by You to live it.

In Your name, Amen.

Gunner

# Prayer For A Friend

### For: John Morris Artist, author, artist.
### www.johnmorrisartfromtheheart.com

Dear Heavenly Dog Father,

I had a friend when I was a pup
A friend of mine was he

We would laugh, sing, play fetch in the sun
That was a great life for me.

I was there when he would fall,
To brighten up his day
I would lick his hand when I could
To chase his fears away.

As the days went by, we grew and grew
And had many happy times
I saw the years jump on quick
And something in me changed.

One night his tears did flow
As he cuddled my head
I love you, my dear friend
From now until the end.

The next day it was time
So my dear friend said
We went for a ride to the vet
And laid me upon a bed.

He looked into my eyes
And sleepy did I feel.
Then something strange happened to me
I really did not seem real.

The next I knew, all around
Was new and fresh to see.
Fields of green and skies of blue
Now awaited me.

So here I'll end my poem for my friend
And here I shall ever be
Until it's time that he comes home
To love and join with me.
Love,
 Lucy

# **Dedicated To Sharon,**
**Wife of Damion,**
**Devoted Mother of DJ, Sister to Mel**
**(Who passed away last year from colon cancer)**

Dear Heavenly Dog Father,

BENJI Here

I'm there for you!

No matter what you're going through.

Even if I don't perform, or behave, the way

My canine brothers or other tougher

guard dogs do.

I can still adore you!

Even when you send me to the cage

when I go through that crazy stage

of listening to my instincts

instead of doing exactly what

you told me not to do.

I don't hold it against you

Because even though I'm SMALL

In status, lick, and bark,

the biggest thing I pray for daily

is that God continues to give me the strength of Sharon's hug
To unconditionally love
You, DJ, and Mel-
And with that love
protect you guys' hearts!
 -Benji

-PS. Bark! Bark! Bark!
(Interpretation by Mel)

# Who Could Turn Down A Face Like That?

The following songs were written by my dear friend and soul sister, Julie Rashell Richmond, especially for the Heavenly Dog Father Prayer Book. Julie wants all proceeds to go for saving dogs. The lyrics are on the following pages, and you can buy the entire songs on my website, <authorlaramagallon.com>. Julie has been a professional singer/songwriter since she was a child and wrote and performed for and with many notable artists and entertainers.

**Who Could Turn Down A Face Like That?**

Who could turn down

A face like that

Who could refuse

The little they ask

I made a vow

When I took you home

You'd never go back

To a place like that

You gave me love

Like i've never known

When I'm sad and feel alone

You're always there

By my side

A truer friend

I could never find

Who could turn down

A face like that

Who could refuse

A homeless pet

They'll win your heart

And you won't regret

That you feel in love

WIth a face like that

Composed by Julie Rashell Richmond

Publisher House of Destiny Music BMI

# Christmas Paws

Snow is falling on the ground
As Christmas time grows near
Will Santa bring a puppy
For boys and girls this year
Some may come from pet shops
You see in shopping malls
But what about the puppies
Forgotten at the pounds

Will Christmas Paws
And Santa Claus
Come to your house this year
Hang an extra stocking
Just in case you hear
A little bark to welcome you
On Christmas day.
And with some love Christmas Paws
Just might come to stay

Some have tails that are short
Some have tails real long
With coats of many colors
Sizes large and small

Different personalities looking for a home
And someone to love them
So they won't be alone

Will Christmas paws
And Santa Claus
Come to your house this year
Hang an extra stocking
Just in case you hear
A little bark to welcome you
On Christmas day
And with some love Christmas Paws
Just might come to stay

And with some love Christmas Paws
Will make your Christmas day

Composed by Julie Rashell Richmond
Copyright by House of Destiny Music

"What the caterpillar calls the end of the world,

the master calls a butterfly. "

— Richard Bach

www.ingramcontent.com/pod-product-compliance
Lightning Source LLC
LaVergne TN
LVHW041708060526
838201LV00043B/637